Martin Rambach

Silicon China, a country of boundless opportunity?

A portrayal of China's technological and societal development ambitions

Bibliografische Information der Deutschen Nationalbibliothek:

Die Deutsche Nationalbibliothek verzeichnet diese Publikation in der Deutschen Nationalbibliografie; detaillierte bibliografische Daten sind im Internet über http://dnb.d-nb.de abrufbar.

Impressum:

Copyright © Science Factory 2018

Ein Imprint der Open Publishing GmbH, München

Druck und Bindung: Books on Demand GmbH, Norderstedt, Germany

Covergestaltung: Open Publishing GmbH

"When the wind of change blows,
some build walls while others build windmills."

European proverb used by Li Keqiang, 7th premier of the State Council of the People's Republic of China at the World Economic Forum 2015 in Davos, Switzerland.

TABLE OF CONTENTS

ACKNOWLEDGEMENTS .... **VI**

ABSTRACT .... **VII**

LIST OF ABBREVIATIONS .... **VIII**

LIST OF FIGURES .... **IX**

LIST OF TABLES .... **IX**

1 PREFACE 1

2 Made in China 2025 4
    2.1 Background 4
    2.2 Main content 5
    2.3 Threats and Limitations 11

3 HIGH TECHNOLOGY FROM THE MIDDLE KINGDOM 13
    3.1 Future of mobility 14
    3.2 E-commerce and Financial technology 17
    3.3 Artificial Intelligence 20

4 CHINA AND THE WESTERN WORLD 23
    4.1 Chinese influence on Europe 23
    4.2 China, the United States and the new tech world order 26

5 THE SOCIETAL PERSPECTIVE 29
    5.1 Internet in China 29
    5.2 The Social Credit System 31

6 METHODOLOGY 34

7 INTERPRETATION OF RESULTS 36

8 CONCLUSION 39

9 REFERENCES 41

ACKNOWLEDGEMENTS

I would like to take this opportunity to thank all the people that have helped me throughout my studies of European Business and who had helped me in my efforts to conduct research for my bachelor thesis.

I would particularly express my gratitude to my supervisor, Prof. Dr. Sean Patrick Saßmannshausen, Professor for Business Administration and Academic Director of the Start-Up Center, for all his precious advice, recommendations and support he provided.

Finally, I would to thank my friends, fellow students and family for their help, encouragement and support during my studies of European Business

ABSTRACT

For decades, the People's Republic of China has made a giant leap from a backward agricultural state to the largest manufacturer in the world. But in recent years, the Chinese government has realized that it is time for a so-called rejuvenation of its great nation. For the most part, the reforms are summarized in the industrial policy Made in China 2025. The goal is no longer just to be the workbench of the world, but also to catch up to other industrialized countries in terms of quality and efficiency. The country intends to be the world-leading high-tech manufacturer. This ambitious strategy therefore causes changes around the world. The United States of America are disadvantaged by the protectionist tendencies. The states of the European Union are also skeptical about the Chinese plans. Especially when it comes to a possible political influence, which arises from an increased economic dependence.

Western countries should see China's development strategies as a wake-up call with the goal of peaceful coexistence among industrialized states.

LIST OF ABBREVIATIONS

GDP	Gross Domestic Product
China/PRC	People's Republic of China
MIC 2025	Made in China 2025
e.g.	exempli gratia/for example
i.e.	id est/that is
MIIT	Ministry of Industry and Information Technology
ICT	Information and communications technology
IP	Intellectual property
NEV	New energy vehicle
PPP	Purchasing power parity
IoT	Internet of Things
IoV	Internet of Vehicles
Fintech	Financial technology
BaFin	Federal Financial Supervisory Authority ("**B**und**es**anstalt für **Fin**anzdienstleistungsaufsicht")
FDI	Foreign direct investment

LIST OF FIGURES

Figure 1: GDP per capita in USD (left axis) and demographic development in m. (right axis), 2017 2

Figure 2: Political system of the People's Republic of China (simplified, author's own illustration) 5

Figure 3: Chronology of the State Council's Plan (author's own illustration) 7

Figure 4: Vulnerability of selected industrial countries to Made in China 2025 7

Figure 5: Industry aims of Made in China 2025 for the domestic market share of Chinese products 9

Figure 6: Level of automation of the PRC's industry measured by density of industrial robots per 10,000 workers in 2015 11

Figure 7: Labor productivity in selected countries (GDP per employee, constant 2011 PPP in USD) 12

Figure 8: Number of patent applications in the PRC (2000-2016) 13

Figure 9: Development of battery cost and battery energy density (2008-2022) 16

Figure 10: Comparison of Chinese (red) and Western (yellow) E-commerce firms by market capitalization in 2018 17

Figure 11: Online payment services in China (red) and United States (yellow), users in million, 2018 19

Figure 12: Fundraising by Chinese artificial intelligence startups 21

Figure 13: Selected Chinese AI firms, projects and cooperations 22

Figure 14: Transaction volume of takeovers and capital participation in Europe in Million US-Dollar 23

Figure 15: China's due diligences and equity participation in Germany (2010-2017) 25

Figure 16: United States-China Trade Balance of goods (2007-2016) in billion US-Dollar 27

Figure 17: Internet users and methods of internet access in million, internet coverage in percent 30

Figure 18: Pilot projects of the Chinese social credit system 32

Figure 19: The phases of the used qualitative research design 35

Figure 20: The mechanism pf a SWOT analysis 36

Figure 21: SWOT analysis on China's leadership ambitions 37

LIST OF TABLES

Table 1: The ten priority sectors.. 8

Table 2: The core of development of the Connected Car industry 16

1 PREFACE

Over eighteen out of the last twenty centuries have been dominated by China like no other country before. Only the last two centuries can be stated as exceptions (Zakaria *et al.* 2011). But in those eighteen centuries before, China was not a strongly interconnected economic power as it is today. As the Middle Kingdom, the Chinese people saw themselves as the center of the world. Not just as a great civilization, but as the civilization par excellence. Both the splendid isolation and the pursuit of hegemony crumbled in the 19th century, when Western European nations made their way to China with their fleets. The earlier industrialization in Europe and the technical progress combined with economic ambitions made this necessary. The Chinese, until then had only diplomatic relations with other countries to confirm their own Chinese primacy. Subsequently, Middle Kingdom experienced severe shocks from Europeans who tried to impose a world order that was completely incompatible with the traditional Chinese ideology. From this time onwards, the country lost its top position (Kissinger 2012).

This decline in power and weakness should therefore be an example of something that should never happen again for the Chinese civilization. Thus, in 1949, the People's Republic of China was founded based on a socialist system. At that time, GNP per capita was still below the level of 1820. However, this soon changed. After the time under Mao Zedong and its partially unsuccessful economic initiatives (including Cultural Revolution), Deng Xiaoping took power in 1978 (Paul and Liqin 2011). According to his maxim "It does not matter if a cat is black or white, as long as it catches mice." the political orientation of the individual was no longer decisive in contrast to Mao Zedong. From this time onwards, the efficiency and capability of the people under a socialist order were in the foreground (Meisner 1996). Deng's reform plans, which provided an economic opening, had great importance on the rapid development of the Chinese economy in subsequent decades (Paul and Liqin 2011).

This situation is illustrated in Figure 1 by the nominal GDP per capita growth in USD from 1960 to 2017 and the growing population from 1950 to 2017. Regarding GDP per capita, which raised from $307.8 (1978) to $7329.10 in 2017. This represents an increase of 2381.12 percent. Furthermore, the population growth has grown by 251.8 percent to $1390.1 billion in 2017 (TradingEconomics.com; 2017).

In these years, China has evolved from a backward agrarian to a flourishing nation as one of the most important players in world trade. Nowadays China is considered to be the so-called workbench of the world (Kissinger 2012).

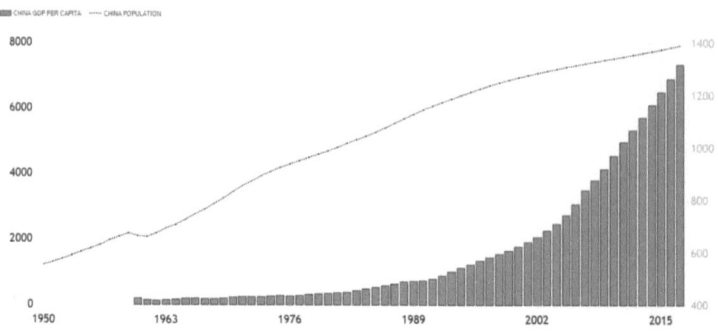

Figure 1: GDP per capita in USD (left axis) and demographic development in m. (right axis), 2017

However, this economic development is not enough for the Middle Kingdom. For some years, Chinese politicians have been increasingly seeking a global, political leadership claim in the world. As in late October 2017, Xi Jinping, 7th President of People's Republic, announced the beginning of a new era of Chinese-style socialism. China should face a great future and the great rejuvenation of the Chinese nation (Dorloff 2018). Among other things, the government of China wants to achieve this through the Belt and Road Initiative (until 2016: One Belt, One Road), which aims to strengthen economic connections between China and the European Economic Union through massive direct investment (Swaine 2015).

However, the Chinese state still has one more goal: to gain technological supremacy (Wübbeke *et al.* 2016). For this reason, the strategy paper *Made in China 2025* was introduced in 2015. The efforts to achieve those ambitions represent the research question and are analyzed in this thesis.

First, the project's political dimension and the Made in China 2025 plan published by the State Council are discussed.

In the following chapter, a more economic component is being discussed and analyzed focusing on the Chinese high-tech industries of Artificial Intelligence, Mobility, E-commerce, financial technology and its involved major players.

In addition, the international perspective of the Chinese development ambitions is considered and potential implications for other countries are presented. In this context, the main focus lies on the United States of America and the European Union.

Likewise, the thesis also addresses the Chinese government's socio-economic development plans of recent years regarding the Internet, data protection and the social credit system.

The final synthesis critically considers all technological and societal development ambitions and, based on this, gives a possible outlook in the future.

2 MADE IN CHINA 2025

2.1 Background

China is a country of sheer size. With a population of approximately 1.4 billion people, it is the most populous country in the world (refer to figure 1). Today, one fifth of the world's population lives on Chinese soil. More than 6 million people live in each of China's eleven most populous cities. Compared to the European Union, this is a giant idea of size. In the EU there is only one comparable city: London. Furthermore, eleven of the 27 member states of the EU do not reach the mark of 6 million inhabitants (Zakaria et al. 2011).

All of this is based on a "unitary one-party socialist republic" in which the Communist Party of the People's Republic of China has an absolute power monopoly.

As can be seen in figure 2, apart from the Communist Party, there is a formally equally important part of the system of government: the state. These two parts have strong internal links. One example is the office of President of the People's Republic of China, which has been run by Xi Jinping since 2012. As head of state, the president possesses representative functions, compared to the German Federal President.

Since 1993, the president of State has additionally held the position of *General Secretary of the Communist Party*. Furthermore he serves as *Chairman of the Central Military Commission*, commander-in-chief of the world's largest military forces (Heilmann 2016). This makes him the head of party and state to the country's most powerful politician, considered as paramount leader for life (Lam 2018).

The constitution's highest organ of state power is the *National People's Congress*. This approximately 3,000-member parliament meets once a year and is responsible for amendments and the drafting of laws. Ahead of the German Bundestag, it is the parliament with the largest parliamentary body in the world. More than two-thirds of the delegates belong to the

Communist Party. The other third is divided into eight different small parties of minor importance. Due to the size of the National People's Congress, the *Standing Committee* acts as de facto legislative and therefore ratifies the majority of the laws. The tasks of the executive, comparable to a central government, are owned by the *State Council of the People's Republic of China* with its 36 members (2018). As the "highest organ of the state administration", it includes the Cabinet and the highest chairmen of the country's top institutions. The executive position holds the prime minister, who is thus seen as the highest man in the state after the president (Heilmann 2016).

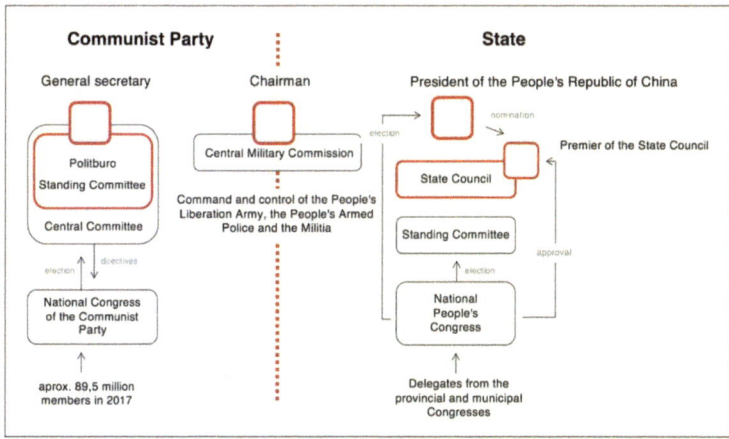

Figure 2: Political system of the People's Republic of China (simplified, author's own illustration)

2.2 Main content

> "Be not afraid of growing slowly; Be afraid only of standing still."
> *Chinese Proverb*

As a socialist nation, the People's Republic of China relies on a centrally planned economy combined with market economy principles. The Chinese government calls this "socialist market economy" (Fischer, D. 2006). A typical planned economic initiative is the five-year plan, which sets the general economic strategy of a country for five ongoing years. Such a strategy paper was last published in PRC in 2016 (Wang 2016). However, there are also stated initiatives that are even more important by creating dynamism that affects the entire globe. This type of strategy paper is *Made in China 2025* (MIC 2025) or also called China Manufacturing 2025.

Unveiled by Li Keqiang in 2015, it summarizes a wide range of technological development ambitions of the Chinese state. Priority has a 10 year plan until 2025 (Institute for Security & Development Policy 2018). It was devised by the Ministry of Industry and Information Technology (MIIT) for two and a half years in collaboration with 150 experts from the China Academy of Engineering (Kennedy 2015). As you can see in figure 3, the strategy also includes steps that go further until the 100th anniversary of the PRC in 2049 (Georgiou Daniel and Hui Xu 2018).

The central goal of the plan is to establish China as the world's high-tech superpower. The state wants to replace the image "Made in China", which has been suggesting for decades low-cost manufactured goods. Through the strategy, the PRC wants to gain global importance for quality, productivity and innovation, rather than for volume manufacturing (China-Britain Business Council 2016).

The plan contains a similarity to the 2013 adopted German initiative "Industry 4.0". However, the Chinese approach is much broader (Kennedy 2015).

It aims to significantly improve the global value chain (State Council of the People's Republic of China 2015). This inevitably means competition for established industrialized countries of the world, which are pioneers in these sectors (Wübbeke 2015).

Step one: to be achieved by 2025
- Comprehensively upgrade China's manufacturing sectors
- Strengthen China's position as a major manufacturing nation
- Focus on quality manufacturing and smart manufacturing technologies
- Improve the efficiency of energy, labour and material consumption
- Make Chinese companies leader in the manufacturing value chain
- Master key technologies in key industries (as opposed to importing them)

Step two: to be achieved by 2035
- Raise China to the level of a mid-ranking manufacturing nation
- Increase innovation
- Increase IP ownership
- Achieve globally innovative breakthroughs in key sectors

Step three: to be achieved by 2049
- Become a global leader in key high-end manufacturing sectors
- Drive innovation and hold competetive advantages

Figure 3: Chronology of the State Council's Plan (author's own illustration)

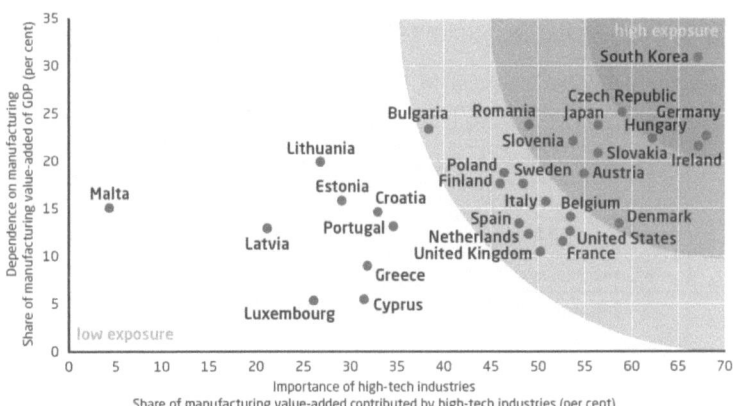

Figure 4: Vulnerability of selected industrial countries to Made in China 2025

Figure 4 illustrates this issue by the relationship between the share of manufacturing value-added GDP in percent and the share of high technology in manufacturing value-added in percent. The chart shows above-average values of both indicators, especially for large industrialized nations, such as South Korea, Germany or Japan. The United States, the largest industrial power in the world, and a large number of European countries are also in the mid-exposure range (Wübbeke *et al.* 2016, p.6).

The ambitions on the way to a world-leading manufacturing power should be achieved with continuous replacement of foreign high-tech products and services by domestic innovation and manufacturing (China-Britain Business Council 2016). This automatically reduces the chances of foreign companies and investors in the Middle Kingdom. Such protectionist tendencies are pervasive within the Chinese economic system. For example, the automotive industry does not allow foreign direct investments (FDI) without a Chinese collaboration partner. In practice, a foreign investor is forced to establish a joint venture in which the Chinese company holds a majority stake (Bölinger 2018).

The Chinese state will focus on ten high-tech sectors in *Made in China 2025*, which are visualized in table 1 (European Chamber of Commerce in China 2017).

Next generation information technology
High-end numerical control machinery and robotics
Aerospace and aviation equipment
Maritime engineering equipment and high-tech maritime vessel manufacturing
Advanced rail equipment
Energy-saving vehicles and new energy vehicles (NEVs)
Electrical equipment
Agricultural machinery and equipment
New materials
Biopharmaceuticals and high-performance medical services

Table 1: The ten priority sectors

In some of those sectors, such as information and communications technology, the PRC already has a worldwide reputation and extensive dominance through the rapid development of **B**aidu, **A**libaba, **T**encent (BAT) and Huawei. Also in the field of high-end numerical control machinery and robotics, China already has solid success. Since 2002, China has been in the vanguard of the world's largest machine tool manufacturers. However, the country still has a strong dependency on core components, which are mostly imported from industrialized countries (China-Britain Business Council 2016). As we have seen in figure 5, the Chinese government aims at an increase in the domestic market share of Chinese products of several sectors (Institute for Security & Development Policy 2018).

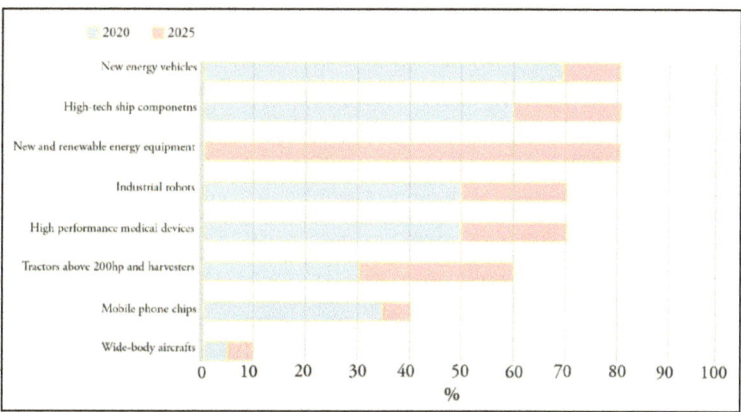

Figure 5: Industry aims of Made in China 2025 for the domestic market share of Chinese products

As the third priority sector, the aviation industry has been selected. This sector already achieves success. China is home to many manufacturing bases of global players, for instance to the two leading aircraft manufacturers Boeing and Airbus. For the year 2020, the PRC aims for its own competitive and complete aircraft manufacturing industry to manufacture its own medium-sized helicopters, high-end business jets and emergency aircraft. Moving up the value chain is also the core objective in maritime engineering equipment. In the advanced rail equipment sector, the Middle Kingdom holds significant intellectual property (IP) in the production of high-speed train manufacturing technology. The government is therefore targeting so-called intelligent transportation systems (ITS) in MIC 2025, which make trains safer and more environmentally friendly (China-Britain Business Council 2016).

As the world leader in the production of battery cells with a share of 37 percent in 2016, China is also well positioned in the field of energy-saving and new energy vehicles (NEVs). In 2020, China aims to reach a share of 64 percent with massive subsidies for customers of locally-produced new energy vehicles (Dahlmann 2018)s. The government also has prescribed as the world's first country a 30 percent minimum share of electric or hybrid vehicles for all government vehicles. In the field of agricultural machinery and technology, the PRC lacks a large number of advanced technologies and is therefore dependent on imports, similar to the numerical control machinery. Therefore, it concentrates on the raising of capabilities in the smart manufacturing of farming equipment. Finally, the government intends to do research in the new material sector. The core element is the development of "functional performance metals, artificially synthesized high-end polymers, inorganic non-metallic materials and high-performance composites".

The ten priority sectors are accompanied by five major initiatives when it comes to the implementation, which can be seen on the next page. The plan identifies the goal of raising domestic content of core components and materials to 40 percent by 2020 and 70 percent by 2025 (China-Britain Business Council 2016).

- establish 15 new innovation centers by 2020 and 40 centers by 2025
- establish four new national research bases
- implement projects focusing on smart manufacturing
- implement projects focusing on green manufacturing
- prioritize high-end equipment manufacturing in key sectors

2.3 Threats and Limitations

The approach is similar in theory to a ground-breaking technological manifest. *Made in China 2025* is a governmental approach to a clear top-down strategy of the Chinese central government, fueled by massive subsidies and investments in their own economy. At the same time, they make it more difficult for foreign companies to make profitable and efficient investments (Duesterberg 2017).

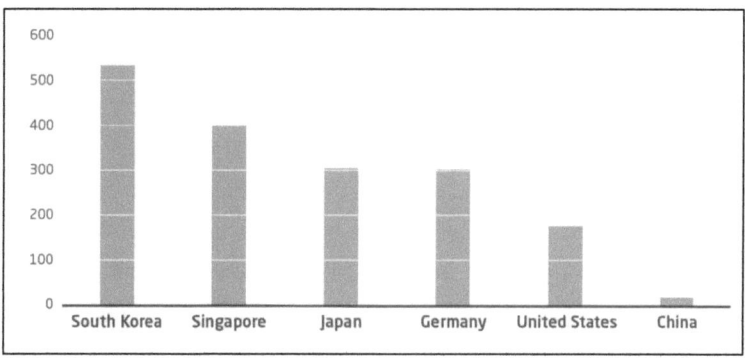

Figure 6: Level of automation of the PRC's industry measured by density of industrial robots per 10,000 workers in 2015

In addition, the backwardness of the Chinese economy in terms of automation and digitalization should not be overestimated. Chinese companies are regarded as reluctant and highly risk-adverse in manufacturing compared to new technology firms from other countries. Figure 6 shows the level of automation measured by the amount of industrial robots per 10,000 industry employees within Chinese companies in 2015. China's represents a massive development backlog regarding its 19 industrial robots per 10,000 workers, in contrast to industrial nations like for example South Korea (531), Germany (301) and United States (176) (Wübbeke *et al.* 2016).

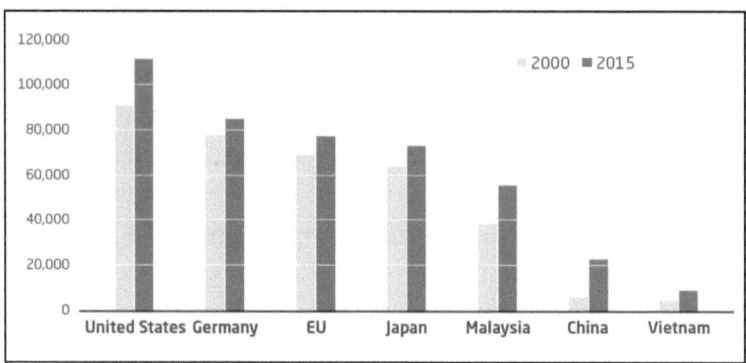

Figure 7: Labor productivity in selected countries (GDP per employee, constant 2011 PPP in USD)

It is certain that not only the number of industrial robotics per 10,000 industrial employees, but also e.g. the labor productivity is an important asset to a country. According to figure 7, however, the PRC shows great weaknesses in the comparison of labor productivity to other industrialized countries. It is questionable whether such differences can be made up in a few years. Another difficulty is the cost pressure, its manufacturing industry faces from two sides by more industrialized countries e.g. Germany or South Korea and low-cost manufacturing nations e.g. other BRICS countries (BRICS: **B**razil, **R**ussia, India, **C**hina, **S**outh Africa). This makes an effective strategy difficult to implement (Wübbeke *et al.* 2016).

3 HIGH TECHNOLOGY FROM THE MIDDLE KINGDOM

> "You should learn from your competitor,
> but never copy. Copy and you die."
>
> *Jack Ma, founder and executive chairman of The Alibaba Group*

China is the second largest economy in the world. By using a mercantilist industrial policy with high state-supported investments combined with low domestic wages rates, it has made China the world's largest trading nation (Duesterberg 2017). As discussed in the previous chapter, the following chapter wants to seek the path to innovation-driven digital power. A meaningful indicator is the development of patent applications in recent years, which is shown in figure 8 (Münchrath *et al.* 2018). As a result, the PRC has succeeded in dethroning the European Union and the United States, and even taking the lead, by continuously increasing it. Among other things, the country owes this dominance to its 164 unicorns (2018), young privately held companies valued at over $ 1 billion. This puts China in top ranking position ahead of the United States (Mercator Institute of China Studies 2018). The following section discusses a wide range of companies holding cutting-edge technology.

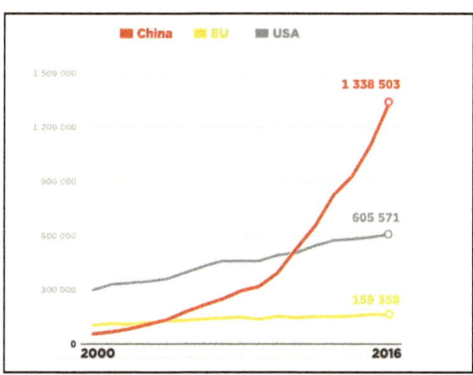

Figure 8: Number of patent applications in the PRC (2000-2016)

3.1 Future of mobility

One of those industries is the automotive and mobility industry. With 29 million vehicles produced in 2017 and therefore a 29.8 percent share of the world's automobile sales, the Chinese automotive market is the largest in the world ahead of the United States (17m) in 2009. According to the *Organisation Internationale des Constructeurs d'Automobiles* (OICA), this means a fourteen-fold increase in absolute terms since the turn of the millennium. The Chinese vehicle market is developing rapidly (Lee, A. 2018). However, in the volume segment of smaller vehicles as well as in the upper class, a strong dominance of Western manufacturers can be seen, even while applying Chinese governmental restrictions, such as the joint venture coercion.

The German premium brands Daimler, BMW and Audi have a market share of 70 to 80 percent in the luxury class and two-thirds of the small cars (Zand 2015). But according to the Chinese government the times of Western dominance are over (Fasse *et al.* 2018). This technological change can be seen in the example of electro-mobility. At the 2018 Beijing Motor Show, 17 percent of the featured vehicles had an electric drive. 71 percent of those vehicles were conceptualized and assembled by Chinese manufacturers. According to the *China Association of Automobile Manufacturers*, the number of electric vehicles (EVs) sold will be 770,000 units in 2017, making the People's Republic the largest market for electric vehicles. In 2018, sales of 1 million NEVs are expected, compared to 400,000 units in the USA (Lee, A. 2018). Accordingly, the PRC is taking advantage of the emerging electro-mobility and increasing digitalization. More specifically, there are young start-ups and technology-driven firms that take advantage of the situation with massive support from the Chinese state in the form of tax relief (Fasse *et al.* 2018).

There is an up-and-coming number of so-called "Tesla Challengers". In addition to increased use of electric drive, those companies share the widespread use of new technologies such as Internet connectivity (Dai 2018). The former battery company BYD (**B**uild **Y**our **D**reams) is market leader in China with sales volumes of 109,485 electric vehicles in 2017. Geely, for example, also achieved great importance in 2018, when it became the largest sole shareholder of the German premium manufacturer Daimler at almost 10 percent. Due to the relatively simple construction in contrast to a combustion drive, the entry barriers to electric mobility have become smaller. This can be recognized by the example of Nio or Byton. Both are young start-ups with promising know-how and a premium claim. Byton's CEO is a former chief developer of BMW's i8 hybrid sports car (Fasse *et al.* 2018). Both companies position themselves as competitors to Tesla as well as BMW, Daimler and Audi. Furthermore, Nio is backed by Chinese internet giants like Tencent, Baidu or Alibaba as investors. In December 2017 the company presented its first model (Campbell 2018). It intends to go public by 2019 on the New York Stock Exchange (Dai 2018).

However, what sets Chinese automakers and brands apart from other manufacturers is their speed of digitalization in the automotive industry. The Chinese government calls this Internet of Vehicles (IoV), based on the Internet of Things (IoT), internetworking of physical devices. This means a technically advanced form of connected cars as technological ecosystem within the vehicle. This gives them the opportunity to prepare strategically well for competitors from other countries and to strengthen competitiveness (Meissner and Wübbeke 2016). Table 2 highlights the seven core elements of connected car features based on the *PwC Industry Bluebook: China Automotive Market: Witnessing the Transformation* (Liu *et al.* 2017).

The competitive advantage of the Chinese automotive industry with regard to digitalization is widespread state promotion of technology firms e.g. smartphone manufacturer Foxconn and insurance company Pingan (Meissner and Wübbeke 2016).

Autonomous driving	Traveling automatically without manual operation
Safety	Ability to warn of road safety and avoid potential collisions
Entertainment	Entertainment functions (WLAN, social network connector, mobile office)
Health	Electronic alert functions optimizing driver's health
Vehicle management	Minimizing operating costs and improves comfort (e.g. traffic data transmission)
Mobility management	Energy efficient driving
Family integration	Ability to connect the vehicle to home, office or other buildings

Table 2: The core of development of the Connected Car industry

In addition to digitizing the car, the PRC has a significant market position in the manufacturing of lithium-ion batteries, the heart of electric vehicles (Spring 2016). Figure 9 illustrates the opposite evolution of NEVs and the battery energy density between 2008 and 2022 (US department of Energy)

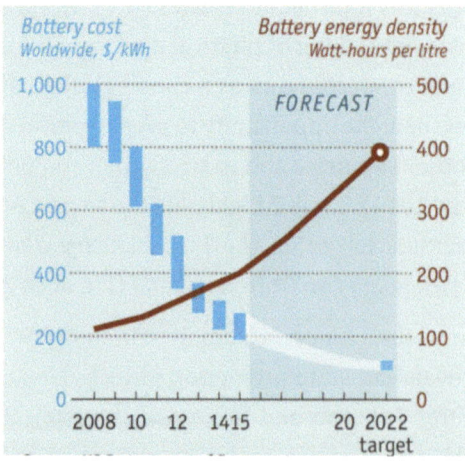

Figure 9: Development of battery cost and battery energy density (2008-2022)

The world market leader in this sector is the Chinese company Contemporary Amperex Technology Limited (CATL). The advantage arose from increased efficiency in production and the securing of raw material reserves. China was able to secure its supply through strategic contracts of Cobalt with the Democratic Republic of Congo. Cobalt is a rare earth metal, essential for the production of batteries and mined by a 60 percent share of world trade in Congo (Steiner 2018).

3.2 E-commerce and Financial technology

Another branch in which the PRC is leading the way with great leaps is e-commerce or also called mobile commerce. Besides, the ever-expanding Chinese middle class is considered as key driver whereas the two major private companies are Alibaba and JD.com (Wübbeke 2014). Founded in 1999, Alibaba dominates China's online trade by 80 percent. In 2014 the company also recorded the largest initial public offering (IPO) in history. With 271 million shares the pricing of the IPO raised $21.8 billion. At that time, the company was comparatively unknown to the Western world despite its ubiquity in China (Baker *et al.* 2014). Figure 10 shows the market capitalization of the largest e-commerce conglomerates of PRC, United States (Amazon) and Germany (Zalando). Tencent owns shares amounting to 20 percent of the enterprise value of JD.com.

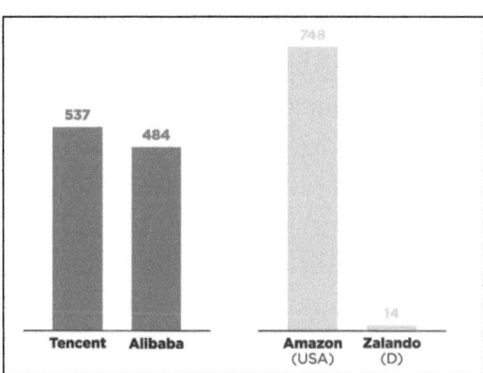

Figure 10: Comparison of Chinese (red) and Western (yellow) E-commerce firms by market capitalization in 2018.

Despite its low market value, the leading Chinese companies are superior to their Western competitors in diverse technologies (Fasse *et al.* 2018). While Amazon is testing the so-called box-less supermarket *Amazon Go* with great publicity in 2018, JD.com has already passed a similar test phase last year. This year the company is therefore on the go to open hundreds of such cash-free supermarkets throughout the country (Kolf and Weddeling 2018).

Alibaba is also revolutionizing commerce by entering new branches of business. Since 2018, the company has been opening a large number of groceries under the name *Hema Fresh*. Its special feature consists of the possibility to have food delivered within 30 minutes by an electric scooter (Fasse *et al.* 2018).

Alibaba and JD.com are taking advantage of the rapidly growing number of Chinese Internet users, amounting to 638 million by 2014 (Wübbeke 2014). Another component of innovation is the creation of partnerships and alliances. As result of this strategy, JD.com forged alliances with real estate developer *China Overseas Land & Investments Ltd.* in order to integrate the company's cash-free markets into smart city projects (Kolf and Weddeling 2018). Smart city is the intelligent networking of municipalities based on ICT and IoT which among other things leads to an increased operational efficiency and share of information with the public, for example by using smart sensors in streetlights (Rouse 2017).

Another partnership of JD.com was founded with its investors Tencent and the world's largest retailer Walmart. The cooperation's purpose comprises a bonus system for clients while effecting a payment to those three companies. The special feature is the use of customer data from the Whatsapp-based App WeChat. In practice, this means: if you make a purchase with the payment function of the social network WeChat, the customer receives a discount. The systematic integration between a trading platform and a payment service provider is less widespread in Western companies, but reality in China.

Alibaba is regarded as archetype of the above-mentioned method. As technology conglomerate, it combines e-commerce with entertainment services like AliMusic, Cloud computing based on Artificial intelligence (AI) like Aliyun and payment platforms like Alipay (Fasse *et al.* 2018). The e-commerce sector is divided into the business-to-business platform

Alibaba, the business-to-consumer platforms Ali Express/Tmall and the largest consumer-to-consumer platform on the internet Taobao. Alibaba therefore has competitors from various sectors, including Amazon for Tmall, Ebay for Taobao and PayPal for Alipay (Schultz *et al.* 2014).

Alipay is the core element of the parent company *Ant Financial Services Group*, founded in 2014. Affiliate company and founder of Ant Financial is Alibaba. In recent years, the foundation has been transformed from an online payment company to a bank-like financial technology (Fintech) firm through launching a money market fund and credit scoring business (Wang 2018). In addition to money transfers through QR codes, the purchase of financial products, the firm allows its clients additionally to raise loans (Fasse *et al.* 2018). With numerous investors and the dynamic evolution of cashless payments in China, Ant Financial's firm value reached $150 billion according to multiple reports by CNBC and Forbes (Wang 2018). Thus, as of August 2018, it is the largest privately-held start up (unicorn) of the world (Pham 2018).

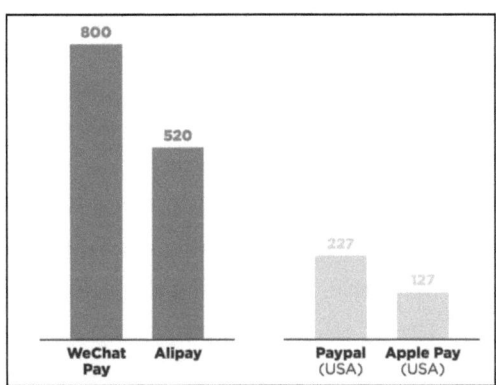

Figure 11: Online payment services in China (red) and United States (yellow), users in million, 2018

Figure 11 illustrates the importance of financial technology in China by the number of users applying online payment services. In this field Alipay is considered market leader due to its clientele of 520 million users. With 800 million users, the Tencent-owned payment solution "WeChat Pay" has nearly four times as many users as the leading US company PayPal. In China, 40 percent of the population use this form of payment. The majority of them every day. In Germany, paying with a smartphone is a rarity. According to a study of the *Bundesbank*, 2 percent of consumers in Germany pay with smartphones. Jan Lukas Korella, policy officer on payments at the *Bundesbank*, sees this situation as a hen-egg problem: there is a lack of consumer demand and therefore a lack of trade and banking investment. There is no causality between both (Fasse *et al.* 2018). Therefrom Chinese companies are making Western innovations such as e-commerce not only usable, they create a significant form of consumer improvement (Schultz 2012). In this context, Jack Ma's quotation from the chapter's beginning can be regarded as maxim for China's technological power on the way to a innovative superpower of the world.

3.3 Artificial Intelligence

Digitalization is omnipresent today. It shapes the everyday life of more and more people on the globe. A significant element of this is Artificial Intelligence (AI). The US think tank Brookings describes this innovation as a "wide-ranging tool that enables people to rethink how we integrate information, analyze data, and use the resulting insights to improve decision-making" (West and Allen 2018). Subsequently the PRC wants to take the lead in this promising field of technology. China wants to become a leader in artificial intelligence (AI) by 2030. This goal is related to Beijing's efforts to make the economy more innovative, to reforming the military service and to gain global influence. The US still has a head start in AI. However, China's ambitions lead to the assessment that there is already a new technology race (Fischer, S.-C. 2018). This is also shown by the following figure through the rapid development of fundraising in AI for startups (Lin 2017).

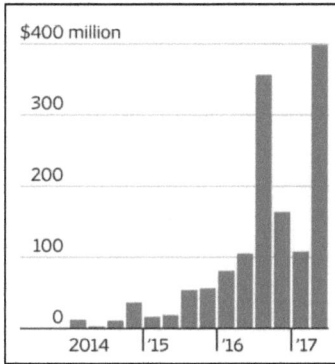

Figure 12: Fundraising by Chinese artificial intelligence startups

In order to make the leap to a innovative economy, China has steadily increased its research and development budget. It has now surpassed the value which has been spent by the US. Furthermore, the Chinese government promotes its targeted high-tech industries such as space, quantum technology and robotics. Reforms have enabled the creation of private technology companies that compete with leading western companies today.

In addition to established companies such as Internet giants e.g. Baidu, Alibaba and Tencent, there is a dynamic start-up scene in China.

The following figure shows numerous projects planned by those Chinese players in AI. These companies are seeking important partnerships alongside with foreign companies. Thus, the Chinese competitor of Uber Didi Chuxing has already build a company base in Silicon Valley with so-called *didi labs*. A similar project is planned by Baidu, Tencent and the startup SenseTime specialized in facial recognition (Fischer, S.-C. 2018).

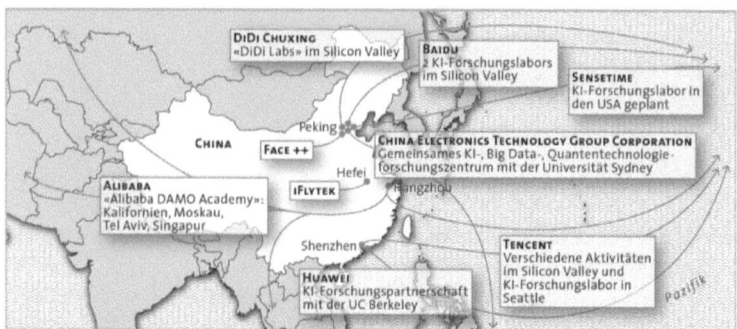

Figure 13: Selected Chinese AI firms, projects and cooperations

Another up-and-coming startup from the Middle Kingdom is iFlytek. Still unknown among Western countries, the company was founded in 1999 by Hu Yu. However, more than 500 million people in China since 2017 have been using the company's voice recognition system based on AI (Sun 2017).

The company dominates the Chinese voice recognition by 80 percent market share. According to an interview, Hu Yu gave to *Handelsblatt*, the company developed the first robot to pass a medical exam a few years ago. He describes the role of the state within China's economy as an important instrument for the economic success of his company (Hua 2018).

4 CHINA AND THE WESTERN WORLD

4.1 Chinese influence on Europe

In 2017 the president of the PRC, Xi Jinping announced the "great rejuvenation of the Chinese nation". An aim which should be implemented through a wide range of development ambitions within China. Therefore, this chapter analyzes the aspirations of the PRC outside its territory. In addition to the Belt and Road Initiative (Swaine 2015), greater willingness for company acquisitions as well as capital participation (Mergers & Acquisitions, M & A) are the main features of this chapter. In this context the following figure shows the development of transaction volume in Europe in USD (Ernst & Young 2018).

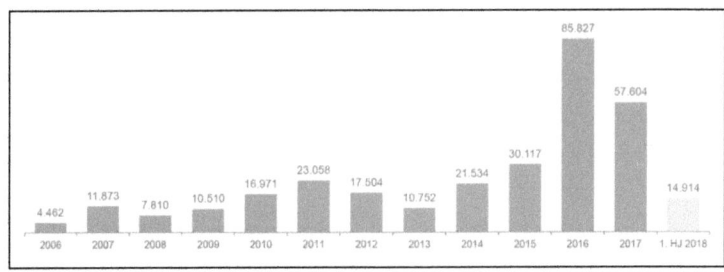

Figure 14: Transaction volume of takeovers and capital participation in Europe in Million US-Dollar

A well-known example is the takeover of the German manufacturer of industrial robots Kuka in early 2017, which was taken over by electrical appliance manufacturer *Midea Group* from Guangdong with an amount of 4.5 billion euros. In recent months, car manufacturer Geely rose now holds 9.7 percent as largest single shareholder of the automotive corporation Daimler (Naß 2018). The transaction was executed through a combination of share purchases and collar options to avoid reporting to the company and the *Federal Financial Supervisory Authority* (BaFin) (Kröner *et al.* 2018). Due to the complexity and large voting rights changes, BaFin intended to investigate the purchase and impose a fine.

Western countries have been confronted with those types of economic influence by the PRC for several years. Sebastian Heilmann, Director of Mercator Institute for China Studies (MERICS) sees the targeted acquisitions as an outflow of know-how aiming at a medium-term replacement of Western technology through Chinese technology. He recommends for an increased protection of domestic technologies through market manipulation practices, similarly to Chinese practices (Naß 2018). Another Chinese influence on European soil could already be observed in 2016 in Greece.

The third Greek aid package of the European Union, which has been adopted as a result of the Greek government-debt crisis, provides privatizations as a condition. The semi-state-owned Chinese shipping company *Cosco* took advantage of these regulations and bought as result of their Belt and Road Initiative the former state port of Piraeus for 280 million euros. This type of Chinese intervention in Greek ans therefore European infrastructure has ambiguous implications. According to the Chinese government, the port is to become the most important port in the Mediterranean, leading to another Greek economic upswing with a flourishing labor market.

However, the influence of politics should not be underestimated. In the past two years, Greek government has voted three times in favor of China and specifically against the EU on European Union summits. This happened with regard to China's human rights policy, territorial disputes in the South China Sea (Spratley Islands conflict) and stricter conditions under which the PRC should invest in the EU. However, a clear link between Chinese investment and Greek decisions cannot be proved. The list of Chinese influence could be expanded. The PRC also bought the largest steel plant in Serbia, a Romanian coal-fired power plant and oil refinery, an Albanian oil field and the international airport of the Albanian capital Tirana (Richter and Ladurner 2017).

The following figure shows the development of Chinese corporate takeover and equity participation in Germany according to the German Economic Institutes in Cologne (IW). The graph confirms the activity of

Chinese investors in Germany, similar to the European perspective in the figure before and shows a slightly increased trend in the quantity of published takeovers and capital participation (Wissenschaftliche Dienste des Deutschen Bundestags 2018).

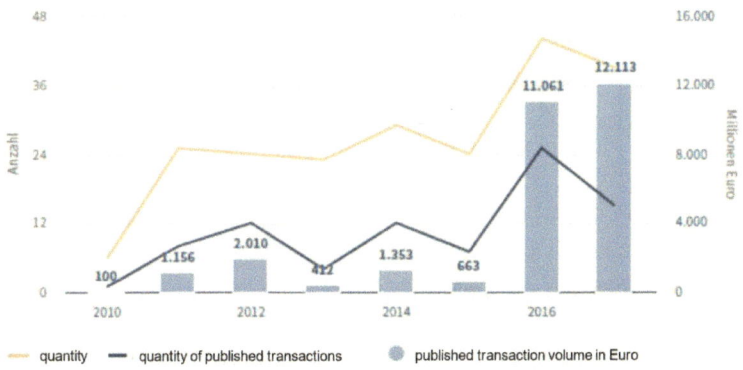

Figure 15: China's due diligences and equity participation in Germany (2010-2017)

However, in contrast to German foreign direct investments (FDI), Chinese investments in Germany are still moderate in the Middle Kingdom. In 2017, German companies invested 70 billion euros, twice as much in the PRC as Chinese firms (30-35 billion euros). However, the increase in Chinese FDI strives to move forward faster, following the strategy paper *Made in China 2025*. Besides China is showing interest in so-called critical infrastructure, sensitive technologies with a high impact on the population. This is demonstrated by the example of *50Hertz*, former called *Vattenfall Europe*. One of the four major transmission system operators for electricity in Germany. The Chinese state-owned company *State Grid Corporation of China* (SGCC) intended to hold a 20 percent stake in the company in early 2018. This project could be prevented by the German government due to a right of first refusal of another Belgian transmission system operator (Naß 2018).

Thus, the Federal Republic of Germany applies as one of the biggest beneficiaries of globalization regulatory policy. However, the PRC operates a similar approach. As mentioned above, there is a joint venture coercion in China, which forces foreign automotive corporations into production partnerships. The corporations are forced to share the profits and know-how of their Chinese locations. Due to the potential 25 percent of import tariffs on automobiles, foreign companies prefer to produce its cars in the Middle Kingdom, as the world's largest auto market. Thus, a similar protectionist approach is the Chinese subsidy policy. For example, battery producers with a capacity of at least eight gigawatt hours must produce in order to receive state subsidies. This number is only achieved by two Chinese manufacturers: CATL and BYD.

In addition, the import licenses for China's food industry have been strengthened so that foreign food manufacturers, in addition to the ingredients, also have to submit far-reaching details about the manufacturing process to the approval authority. A similar list of foreign know-how also requires cyber security law, published in 2017, which forces companies to store data on Chinese servers (Bölinger 2018).

4.2 China, the United States and the new tech world order

The United States of America has been considered an economic and political world power based on the concept of Pax Americana since the 20th century. This also applies to their technological influence around the world. The heart of business, high technology and entrepreneurship in the world lies in a tiny valley embraced by San Francisco Peninsula and between San Mateo and San José: Silicon Valley. But China is on the move. With its offensive industrial policy, it is increasingly becoming a high-tech nation (Kliman and Cooper 2017). In other words: Made in China is competing with Made in America.

The following figure published by US census bureau and Statista illustrates the Sino-American trade balance of goods. You can see a comparatively high trade deficit over the last ten years, which increased over the years. The PRC exports approximately four times the value of goods which the US exports to China.

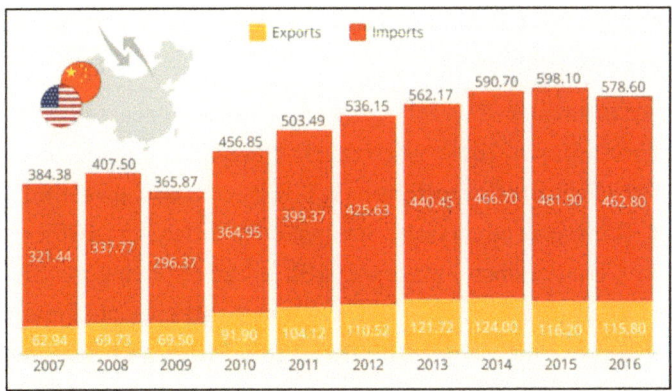

Figure 16: United States-China Trade Balance of goods (2007-2016) in billion US-Dollar

The graph gives a comprehensive overview of the imports and exports of goods with China as the largest goods trading partner of the United States. The key exporting categories to China in 2016 were e.g. agricultural crop soybeans ($ 15 billion), aircraft ($ 15 billion) and electrical machinery ($ 12 billion).

Whereas the key import categories from China in 2016 were e.g. electrical machinery ($ 129 billion), machinery ($ 97 billion), and furniture / bedding ($ 29 billion) (Office of the United States Trade Representative 2016).

The figure does not, however, take into account the tertiary sector of the US economy, including exports and imports of services. The tertiary sector is widely regarded as largest sector of industrialized countries.

In this area, the US has a trade surplus of $38 billion, an increase of 13,6 percent in 2016 compared to 2015. Composed of travel, intellectual property (i.e. trademark, computer software) and transportation, the absolute export value of the US is $ 54,2 billion. According to the United States Trade Representative, this means an increase of more than 11,6 percent in 2015, 412 percent since 2006 and 908 percent greater than 2001 levels.

The government of the United States sees the trade deficit of goods with the PRC of $375 billion as serious issue and therefore wants to greatly reduce it. The Trump Administration sees this as unfair competition. Especially through *Made in China 2025*, the Chinese government is accused of violating IP, enforced technology transfer and political interference by the Communist Party (Naß 2018).

This resulted in a series of so-called "strong actions" addressed China's unfair trade from March 2018 onwards. They include a chain of debates within the World Trade Organization (WTO), 25 percent ad valorem duties on certain Chinese products and investment restrictions (Office of the United States Trade Representative 2018). In the following month, those actions were imposed by the American government. They hold import tariffs of $50 billions for Chinese products (e.g. soybeans) (Gießen *et al.* 2018). In response, the PRC proposes similar actions including 25 percent tariffs on $50 billions of US products including soybeans and beef (Eller 3018). Further punitive tariffs on the part of the United States in the amount of up to $ 250 billions were announced, but not executed. The Chinese government then announced similar procedures "of the same quality and quantity."

However, these governmental measures are particularly damaging the wealth of the American population, which may reckon with diminished demand. This happened in the example after the introduction of punitive tariffs of soybeans as one of the most important American export goods. According to Max Zenglein from MERICS, the American tariff actions only have a braking and therefore short-term effect. It would not stop the technological advance of China. Rather, foreign countries should insist on improved market access in China and stronger IP rights to protect technology from American companies (Sieren 2018).

In addition to all the punitive duties on soybeans and other goods, there must not be neglected that the key driver behind the American regulatory actions is *Made in China 2025*. It is about the question of who takes the lead in the 21st century. Raymond Zhong of The New York Times described this situation as Technology Cold War (Zhong 2018).

5 THE SOCIETAL PERSPECTIVE

5.1 Internet in China

Internet is a worldwide system of interconnected computers carrying a wide range of information (Rouse 2018). Thus, the internet actually contains a freedom of information. But this is not the case in the most populous country in the world: China. Since 1998, the internet has been restricted by the *Golden Shield Project of the Ministry of State Security* (MSS). At least 100,000 employees officially work for the agency. They are concerned with the targeted application of different methods of censorship, which forms the internet to a "Chinese internet". They include e.g. filtering of specific terms, network bandwidth restriction as well as the complete access blocking to internet pages. This system is also known as the *Great Firewall of China*, based on firewall and the Great Wall of China (Delius 2015).

In the last two decades, the PRC has become the country with the highest number of Internet users. The following figure highlights the evolution with additional mention of the methods of internet access and the country's internet coverage in percent. According to the source, the number of Internet users has increased since 2005 by approximately half a billion users to more than 630 billion users. In addition, the most widespread form of use is the smartphone, followed by the PC and notebook (Wübbeke 2014).

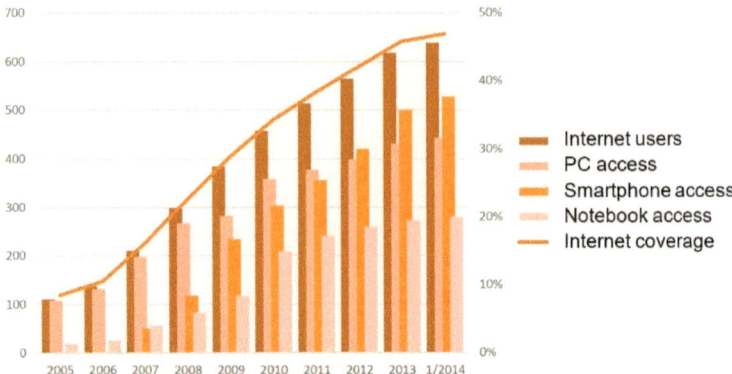

Figure 17: Internet users and methods of internet access in million, internet coverage in percent

However, an increased quantity does not mean increased freedom. On the contrary: The users of the Chinese Internet have less and less access to non-censored messages. According to the Human Rights Report 76 of the Society for Threatened Peoples, this view contradicts Article 19 of the Universal Declaration of Human Rights:

> "Everyone has the right to freedom of opinion and expression; this right includes freedom to hold opinions with- out interference and to seek, receive and impart information and ideas through any media and regardless of frontiers."

(United Nations General Assembly 1948)

In it, the United Nations reaffirm freedom of expression independent of state borders and the associated free choice of media, which should always be respected. In March 2015, a wide range of novel strengthening censorship regulations were adopted. They include restrictions for social networks, blogs, online forums and messaging. Moreover Chinese Internet users are not allowed to foment ethnic conflicts and jeopardize the sovereignty or the territorial integrity (Delius 2015).

According to the Organization Freedom House, China was the world's worst user of internet freedom in 2015. In the same year, the PRC organized a so-called *World Internet Conference* in Wuzhen. Well-known participants were the representatives of Russia, Pakistan and Kyrgyzstan as well as companies like Apple or Google. Xi Jinping campaigned for China's cyber sovereignty and against cyber anarchy in the world wide web (Strittmatter 2015).

In order to achieve those goals, it also has been mandatory since 2015 to register the actual name of each individual Internet user at the respective Internet provider. Chinese authorities are responsible for the complete personal collection of data. All those current censorships pave the way for the Chinese government's long term aim: total surveillance (Delius 2015)

5.2 The Social Credit System

Building on the regulations and restrictions of China's internet, the Chinese state intends cyber sovereignty.

This includes a comprehensive collection of data and their full control and access within a so-called social credit system. The special feature: there is no longer only prohibited and permitted behavior, but much like a computer game: desirable and unwanted behavior. The Chinese reign sees great potential in this kind of gamification as a means to control the behavior of its own citizens. Because unwanted behavior means, in contrast to desired behavior, a deduction of social credit and therefore for the Chinese citizen.

From 2020, this surveillance should help to transform the Chinese society into an Orwellian society. For example, the government of the PRC combines the score of the social credit system with access to state services (Nocun 2018). However, the system has been tested in various Chinese cities since 2015. The following map gives an overview of the pilot projects that the Chinese state intends to introduce in a number of major cities.

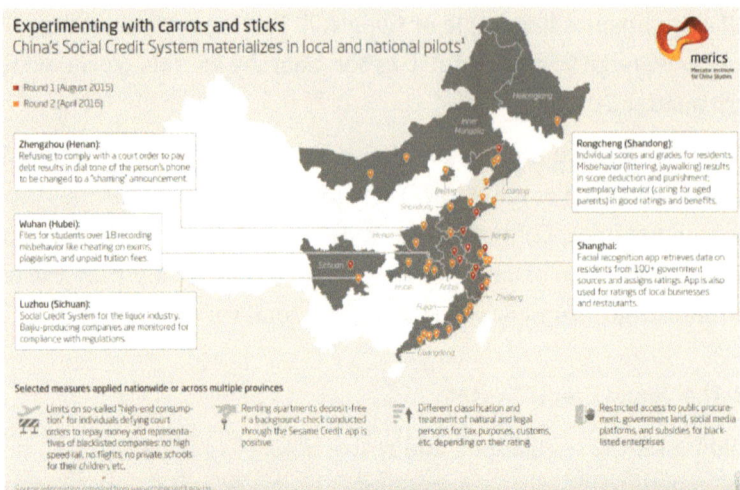

Figure 18: Pilot projects of the Chinese social credit system

Within the illustration, the government of China divides the integration of the social credit system into two phases, which are to be initiated respectively in 2015 and 2016. Shanghai focuses more on facial recognition. Whereas in Wuhan City, the system is being tested within the education system in schools. In Luzhou, on the other hand, the liquor industry is being monitored by the social credit system. Due to the widespread use due to the almost unlimited amounts of data, the social credit system can be extended to all imaginable areas of life (Ohlberg *et al.* 2017).

Whereas e-commerce platforms such as Amazon or Alibaba observe their customers' buying preferences and then submit proposals based on them, the Chinese government acts as a sort of rating agency that can enter in intimate areas of private life.

It is intended that users with at least 1,300 points receive the highest rating AAA. If they can hold this position for some time, they are supposed to receive a discounted loan or better health insurance as reward. Even when awarding study places to one's own children, a high score could have a positive effect. Those who fall below a value of 600, landing in the worst category D, may even fear losing their jobs.

Everyone can find out about their own score via smartphone app. In addition, authorities, banks and employers, landlords should be given access to the evaluation as well (Lee, F. 2017).

However, what the Chinese digital market differentiates from its Western neighbors, is that the Chinese are relaxed with their personal data. Tencent and Alibaba have access to a gigantic pool of data that provides them with real-time information about what their customers are shopping for and where they are. Google or Facebook do that in other countries as well. But China goes much further: the state and ruling Communist Party have access to citizens' data (Shi 2018).

6 METHODOLOGY

Social research (e.g. Business Administration or Economics) in its core has two fundamental methods of research: qualitative and quantitative.

The qualitative research can be described as "an intelligent melting pot of other aspects" because of its property of interpreting different approaches that are integrated in the research task. This implies that a qualitative research is mainly based on reports and findings that are represented in a non-numerical form.

In this context, it is essential to stress that this approach does not require the use of statistics or any numerical data. Therefore, the research work has been conducted from the beginning to the end with a strong focus on meanings. It is of crucial importance for the researcher to understand the issues discussed. The situations are described from the perspectives of the researcher. The design of the research is flexible throughout the research. It requires a small group of individuals involved in the situations under study

Especially due to the timelineness of the research question and due to the absence of usable quantitative data, the portrayal of China's technological and societal development ambitions is based on qualitative research.

In the following figure, the basic phases of the qualitative research done on this topic is being visualized. At the very beginning of every scientific work is the search for a specific research question. It should be noted that the topic has a sufficient number of sources. The substantial basis of the research question builds the initiation of the strategy paper *Made in China 2025*, which was published in 2015.

METHODOLOGY

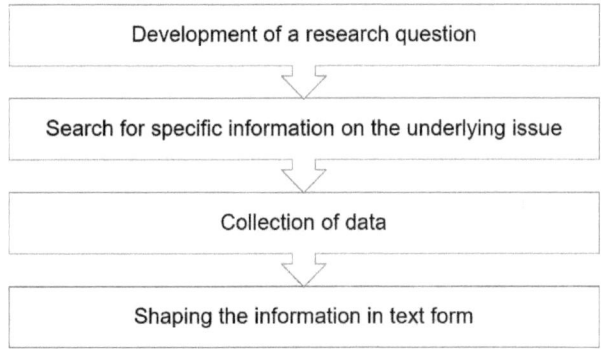

Figure 19: The phases of the used qualitative research design

In the following step, it is necessary to search for suitable sources, which best represent the research question.

It is of great importance that the sources come from different ways of thinking. Especially in the existing research question, it is essential due to the international nature of the topic. In addition, other geographic regions besides China are influenced by the issue. Therefore, a controversial perspective is crucial.

The final step consists of interconnecting and editing the information in text form

7 INTERPRETATION OF RESULTS

China is on the cusp of revolutionizing its key sectors through a wide-range of technological development ambitions. No country in the world is pushing digitalization as consistently as China. The strategy paper *Made in China 2025* outlines the government's route. The goal is to reach a global technology leadership by 2025.

The research question is therefore by what measures the Middle Kingdom wants to rise to a global leadership position when it comes to technology and high-tech innovation. For this reason, a so-called SWOT analysis is used in this scientific work.

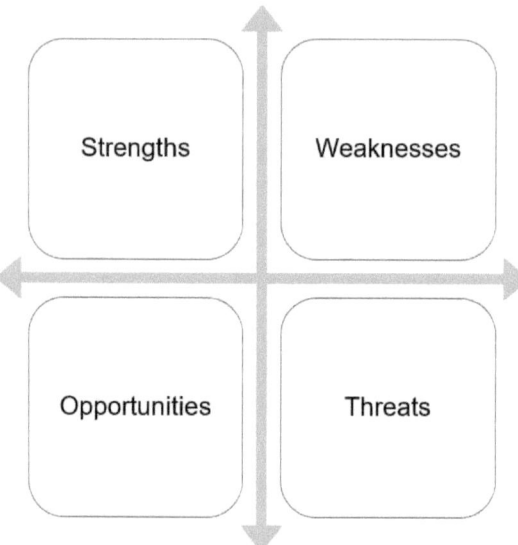

Figure 20: The mechanism pf a SWOT analysis

As you can see in the figure, SWOT is an acronym that stands for Strengths, Weaknesses, Opportunities, and Threats.

Strengths describe the internal positive issues of China's technological development ambitions. Weaknesses are internal aspects of the research question that affect China's ambitions negatively. Opportunities are external factors that explain, why the attributes of China's aims are attractive.

Whereas threats include external factors beyond control that could jeopardize the PRC.

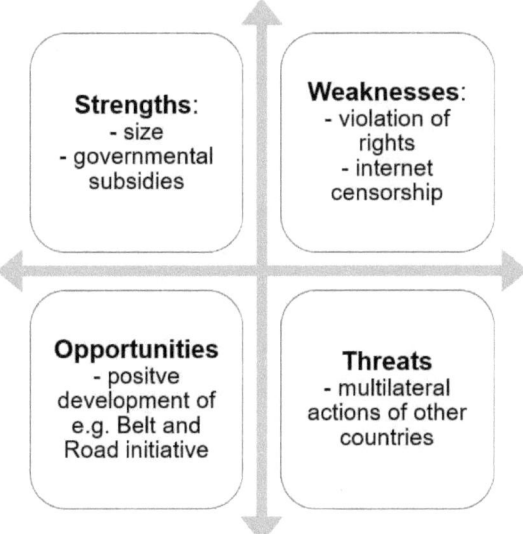

Figure 21: SWOT analysis on China's leadership ambitions

In the case of the Chinese global manufacturing leadership aspirations, creating a SWOT analysis is a complex matter.

However, the sheer size of the country, which is more like a subcontinent, can be considered as strength. The high number of human resources produced by the PRC is unique. The large financial support which the government fosters in companies in the form of subsidies is also a certain success factor. Thus, Chinese companies are vigorously advancing key high technologies such as facial recognition or AI. The high acceptance of new technologies in society and the abundant government subsidies, coupled with the fact that data protection is not considered particularly important by the Chinese. In almost all technology areas today there are so-called "unicorns", young companies that are valued at least $1 billion. China has the largest number of unicorns in the world: 164.

Baidu, Alibaba or Tencent gained global importance and do not longer have an image as copycats in the world. They are seen as innovators and future-makers. Companies like BYD, CATL or Geely are driving forward technical progress - threatening to outstrip Western competition.

Opportunities can be achieved through the successful implementation of the Belt and Road initiative. In part, this can lead to the PRC gaining more economic and political influence in other parts of the world, for example.

Weaknesses are the violation of human rights, which can lead to long-term civil unrest within the population. Censorship of the Chinese internet can also lead to similar dissatisfaction

Finally, threats can be triggered by trade wars. The continuing differences of opinion with the United States can end in such disputes in which both regions have a severe disadvantage.

8 CONCLUSION

There has never been a similar rise in human history. Since the end of 1978, when Deng Xiaoping began economic reforms and opened the People's Republic to the world. Today, China is the largest trading power in the world. The economic boom has changed the Middle Kingdom.

Now digitalization should bring the economy to the top of the world. In the fields of artificial intelligence, quantum computers, big data and autonomous driving, China is powerfully advancing.

However, another thing that should not be underestimated is the restriction of human rights by the initiation of an Orwellian surveillance state and the censorship of the Chinese Internet.

The PRC started buying numerous high-tech companies in Europe and America. Now, they are following the ten-sector state master plan *Made in China 2025*. What initially appeared as an invigorating source of finance, is increasingly turning out to be an economic and political challenge. Everywhere, plans are being forged or laws are being enacted to set technological and security barriers for the Chinese takeover strategy.

China's president of state Xi Jinping does not just want a place in the sun, he wants the absolute top position in all fields. China wants to be the center of the world, once again.

Europe must protect its democracy, its economy and its liberal foundation from harmful Chinese influence. The EU should demand reciprocity. What Western companies are allowed to do in the Western hemisphere should also be allowed in China.

In conclusion, I see the government's intervention in society as the biggest problem of China's rise to a global world power. The ever-increasing process of integration and interaction in the world, also called globalization, will favor the gradual development of similar life philosophies. As soon as the Chinese population learns to grasp those limitations of freedom as a means to an end to the rise of global technology superpower, this, combined with globalization, could lead to a gradual awakening and a not to be underestimated dispute towards the government.

9 REFERENCES

Baker, L.B., Toonkel, J. and Vlastelica, R. (2014). *Alibaba Surges 38 Percent on Massive Demand in Market Debut* [Online]. Available at: https://www.reuters.com/article/us-alibaba-ipo/alibaba-ipo-prices-at-top-of-range-raising-21-8-billion idUSKBN0HD2CO20140919 [Accessed: 29 August 2018].

Bölinger, M. (2018). *China: Das große Mauern* [Online]. Available at: https://www.zeit.de/2018/13/china-protektionismus-xi-jinping-freihandel [Accessed: 23 August 2018].

Campbell, P. (2018). *China's Nio Woos Potential Investors with Ambitious Vision* [Online]. Available at: https://www.ft.com/content/9c78c13e-a13c-11e8-85da-eeb7a9ce36e4 [Accessed: 24 August 2018].

China-Britain Business Council (2016). *Made in China 2025 - China Manufacturing in the 21st Century - Opportunities for UK-China Partnership.* London: China-Britain Business Council.

Dahlmann, D. (2018). *Von einer Abhängigkeit in die nächste – mit Batteriezellen* [Online]. Available at: https://www.gruenderszene.de/automotive-mobility/abhaengigkeit-batteriezellen-deutschland-drehmoment [Accessed: 24 August 2018].

Dai, S. (2018). *Tencent-Backed Tesla Challenger NIO to File Prospectus next Month* [Online]. Available at: https://www.scmp.com/tech/article/2158818/tencent-backed-electric-car-start-nio-file-prospectus-september-planned-us [Accessed: 28 August 2018].

Delius, U. (2015). *Xi Jinpings Große Digitale Mauer - Internetzensur Schürt Menschenrechtsverletzungen in China.* Society for Threatened Peoples.

REFERENCES

Dorloff, A. (2018). *Projekt Weltmacht - Wie China den globalen Aufstieg plant* [Online]. Available at: http://www.deutschlandfunkkultur.de/projekt-weltmacht-wie-china-den-globalen-aufstieg-plant.979.de.html?dram:article_id=407037 [Accessed: 27 May 2018].

Duesterberg, T.J. (2017). The Growing Chinese Threat to Advanced Technology Industries. *Hudson Institute* [Online]. Available at: http://www.hudson.org/research/13825-the-growing-chinese-threat-to-advanced-technology-industries [Accessed: 11 August 2018].

Eller, D. (3018). *China May No Longer Be Buying U.S. Soybeans* [Online]. Available at: http://www.desmoinesregister.com/story/money/agriculture/2018/05/03/report-china-may-no-longer-buying-us-soybeans-trump-trade-war/576481002/ [Accessed: 29 August 2018].

Ernst & Young (2018). *Chinesische Unternehmenskäufe in Europa - Eine Analyse von M&A-Deals 2006-2018.*

European Chamber of Commerce in China (2017). *China Manufacturing 2025 - Putting Industrial Policy Ahead of Market Forces.* Beijing: European Union Chamber of Commerce in China.

Fasse, M., Schneider, K., Scheuer, S., Kolf, F. and Kerkmann, C. (2018). *E-Mobilität, Fintechs, Handel, KI: In diesen Branchen ist China bald unschlagbar* [Online]. Available at: http://www.handelsblatt.com/politik/international/e-mobilitaet-fintechs-handel-ki-in-diesen-branchen-ist-china-bald-unschlagbar/21047476.html [Accessed: 28 May 2018].

Fischer, D. (2006). *Chinas Sozialistische Marktwirtschaft | Bpb* [Online]. Available at: http://www.bpb.de/izpb/8844/chinas-sozialistische-marktwirtschaft?p=all [Accessed: 23 August 2018].

Fischer, S.-C. (2018). *Künstliche Intelligenz: Chinas Hightech-Ambitionen.*

REFERENCES

Georgiou Daniel, O. and Hui Xu, M. (2018). *Made in China 2025: Market Opportunities for EU SMEs.* China-Britain Business Council/EU SME Centre.

Gießen, C., Hagelüken, A. and Mühlauer, A. (2018). *Aus dem Handelsstreit wird ein Handelskrieg* [Online]. Available at: https://www.sueddeutsche.de/wirtschaft/us-strafzoelle-gegen-china-aus-dem-handelsstreit-wird-ein-handelskrieg-1.4017328 [Accessed: 29 August 2018].

Heilmann, S. (2016). *Das politische System der Volksrepublik China.* 3rd ed. Wiesbaden: Springer-Verlag.

Hua, S. (2018). Chinesischer Tech-Pionier Hu Yu: „Wir helfen dem Staat, und er hilft uns". [Online]. Available at: http://www.handelsblatt.com/unternehmen/it-medien/chinesischer-tech-pionier-hu-yu-wir-helfen-dem-staat-und-er-hilft-uns/21047490.html [Accessed: 28 May 2018].

Institute for Security & Development Policy (2018). *Made in China 2025.* Institute for Security & Development Policy.

Kennedy, S. (2015). Center for Strategic & International Studies: Made in China 2025. [Online]. Available at: https://www.csis.org/analysis/made-china-2025 [Accessed: 25 May 2018].

Kissinger, H. (2012). *On China.* 2nd ed. New York City: Penguin Press.

Kliman, D. and Cooper, Z. (2017). *Washington Has a Bad Case of China ADHD* [Online]. Available at: https://foreignpolicy.com/2017/10/27/washington-has-a-bad-case-of-china-adhd/ [Accessed: 29 August 2018].

Kolf, F. and Weddeling, B. (2018). *Kassenloser Supermarkt: Die Zukunft des Einkaufens ist chinesisch* [Online]. Available at: https://www.handelsblatt.com/unternehmen/handel-konsumgueter/kassenloser-supermarkt-die-zukunft-des-einkaufens-ist-chinesisch/20885922.html [Accessed: 29 August 2018].

Kröner, A., Landgraf, R. and Slodczyk, K. (2018). *Bafin untersucht Anteilskauf: Hinter dem Geely-Einstieg bei Daimler steckt ein komplexes Derivategeschäft* [Online]. Available at: https://www.handelsblatt.com/finanzen/anlagestrategie/trends/bafin-untersucht-anteilskauf-hinter-dem-geely-einstieg-bei-daimler-steckt-ein-komplexes-derivategeschaeft/21005084.html [Accessed: 29 August 2018].

Lam, W. (2018). Xi Jinping, Vorsitzender von allem. *Die Zeit* [Online]. Available at: https://www.zeit.de/politik/ausland/2018-05/xi-jinping-china-kommunismus-kommunistische-partei [Accessed: 23 May 2018].

Lee, A. (2018). *China's Electric Car Market Is Growing Twice as Fast as the US. Here's Why* [Online]. Available at: https://www.scmp.com/business/companies/article/2143646/chinas-ev-market-growing-twice-fast-us-heres-why [Accessed: 24 August 2018].

Lee, F. (2017). Die AAA-Bürger. *Die Zeit* [Online]. Available at: http://www.zeit.de/digital/datenschutz/2017-11/china-social-credit-system-buergerbewertung [Accessed: 17 April 2018].

Lin, L. (2017). *China Is Using Facial Recognition to Nab Jaywalkers; Investors Get Interested* [Online]. Available at: https://www.wsj.com/articles/saving-face-investment-in-recognition-technology-heats-up-in-china-1499763603 [Accessed: 30 August 2018].

Liu, W., Shen, S., Jin, J. and Peng, B. (2017). *China Automotive Market: Witnessing the Transformation.* PricewaterhouseCoopers.

Meisner, M.J. (1996). *The Deng Xiaoping Era: An Inquiry into the Fate of Chinese Socialism, 1978-1994.* 1st ed. New York City: Hill and Wang.

Meissner, M. and Wübbeke, J. (2016). Digitalisierung des Autos - Anfang vom Ende des China Booms für internationale Autobauer? *MERICS China Monitor*:7.

Mercator Institute of China Studies (2018). *China Update 7/2018 | Mercator Institute for China Studies* [Online]. Available at: https://www.merics.org/en/newsletter/china-update-72018 [Accessed: 17 August 2018].

Münchrath, J., Hua, S. and Scheuer, S. (2018). *Auf dem Weg zur Internet-Supermacht: Pekings Digital-Plan – Wie China die Technologie-Vorherrschaft übernehmen will* [Online]. Available at: http://www.handelsblatt.com/politik/international/auf-dem-weg-zur-internet-supermacht-pekings-digital-plan-wie-china-die-technologie-vorherrschaft-uebernehmen-will/21047452.html [Accessed: 26 May 2018].

Naß, M. (2018). Chinesische Investitionen: Aufkaufen und ausschlachten. *Die Zeit* [Online]. Available at: https://www.zeit.de/wirtschaft/2018-05/chinesische-investitionen-deutschland-unternehmen-handelsstreit [Accessed: 23 May 2018].

Nocun, K. (2018). *Die Diktatur der Daten* [Online]. Available at: https://www.handelsblatt.com/meinung/kolumnen/expertenrat/nocun/expertenrat-katharina-nocun-die-diktatur-der-daten/20805034.html [Accessed: 17 August 2018].

Office of the United States Trade Representative (2018). *President Trump Announces Strong Actions to Address China's Unfair Trade* [Online]. Available at: https://ustr.gov/about-us/policy-offices/press-office/press-releases/2018/march/president-trump-announces-strong [Accessed: 29 August 2018].

Office of the United States Trade Representative (2016). *U.S.-China Trade Facts* [Online]. Available at: https://ustr.gov/countries-regions/china-mongolia-taiwan/peoples-republic-china [Accessed: 29 August 2018].

Ohlberg, M., Ahmed, S. and Lang, B. (2017). *The Complex Implementation of China's Social Credit System* [Online]. Available at: https://www.merics.org/en/china-monitor/content/5071 [Accessed: 30 August 2018].

Paul, C. and Liqin, C. (2011). *China Verstehen.* 1st ed. Augsburg: Sankt Ulrich Verlag.

Pham, S. (2018). *Chinese Online Payments Giant Could Be Worth $150 Billion* [Online]. Available at: https://money.cnn.com/2018/04/11/technology/ant-financial-services-group-alibaba/index.html [Accessed: 29 August 2018].

Richter, S. and Ladurner, U. (2017). *Habe Geld, suche Einfluss* [Online]. Available at: https://www.zeit.de/2017/39/china-investitionen-einfluss-europa [Accessed: 29 August 2018].

Rouse, M. (2018). *What Is Internet?* [Online]. Available at: https://searchwindevelopment.techtarget.com/definition/Internet [Accessed: 29 August 2018].

Rouse, M. (2017). *What Is Smart City? - Definition from WhatIs.Com* [Online]. Available at: https://internetofthingsagenda.techtarget.com/definition/smart-city [Accessed: 29 August 2018].

Schultz, S. (2012). Internet-Boom: China baut sich sein Silicon Valley. *Spiegel Online* [Online]. Available at: http://www.spiegel.de/wirtschaft/unternehmen/zhongguancun-ist-chinas-silicon-valley-a-815727.html [Accessed: 29 August 2018].

Schultz, S., Braun, K. and Ohdah, D. (2014). Chinas neuer IT-Riese: Das ist Alibaba. *Spiegel Online* [Online]. Available at: http://www.spiegel.de/wirtschaft/alibaba-grafiken-zu-jack-ma-und-chinas-it-konzern-a-989202.html [Accessed: 30 April 2018].

Shi, M. (2018). Die KP liest immer mit. *Die Zeit* [Online]. Available at: https://www.zeit.de/wirtschaft/2018-04/china-digitalisierung-ueberwachung-online-shopping-konsum [Accessed: 25 May 2018].

Sieren, F. (2018). *USA vs China: Ein Technologiekrieg?* [Online]. Available at: https://www.dw.com/de/usa-vs-china-ein-technologiekrieg/a-44391823 [Accessed: 12 August 2018].

Spring, J. (2016). *Power Surge: Chinese Electric Car Battery Maker Charges for Global...* [Online]. Available at: https://www.reuters.com/article/us-china-autos-batteries/power-surge-chinese-electric-car-battery-maker-charges-for-global-market-idUSKBN14E0K1 [Accessed: 28 August 2018].

State Council of the People's Republic of China (2015). *Made in China 2025.*

Steiner, A. (2018). *China ist Europa bei der Batterieproduktion überlegen* [Online]. Available at: http://www.faz.net/1.5691581 [Accessed: 28 August 2018].

Strittmatter, K. (2015). *China will Internet-Zensur zum globalen Standard machen* [Online]. Available at: http://www.sueddeutsche.de/digital/china-grosse-mauer--1.2785391 [Accessed: 25 May 2018].

Sun, Y. (2017). *Why 500 Million People in China Are Talking to This AI* [Online]. Available at: https://www.technologyreview.com/s/608841/why-500-million-people-in-china-are-talking-to-this-ai/ [Accessed: 30 August 2018].

Swaine, M.D. (2015). *Chinese Views and Commentary on the "One Belt, One Road" Initiative.* Hoover Institution.

United Nations General Assembly (1948). *Universal Declaration of Human Rights.*

Wang, N. (2016). *Das neue China: Innovation statt Produktion* [Online]. Available at: https://www.tagesspiegel.de/politik/fuenfjahresplan-das-neue-china-innovation-statt-produktion/13060510.html [Accessed: 23 August 2018].

Wang, Y. (2018). *Ant Financial Said To Close $150B Funding Round* [Online]. Available at: https://www.forbes.com/sites/ywang/2018/05/28/ant-financial-said-to-close-150-b-funding-round/#15d42e307dcc [Accessed: 29 August 2018].

West, D.M. and Allen, J.R. (2018). *How Artificial Intelligence Is Transforming the World* [Online]. Available at: https://www.brookings.edu/research/how-artificial-intelligence-is-transforming-the-world/ [Accessed: 29 August 2018].

Wissenschaftliche Dienste des Deutschen Bundestags (2018). Handelsbeziehungen zwischen Deutschland und China. *Wissenschaftliche Dienste des Deutschen Bundestags.*

Wübbeke, J. (2014). Chinas Internetgiganten treiben ‚Mobile Commerce' an und drängen auf globale Märkte. *MERICS China Monitor* **15**.

Wübbeke, J. (2015). *Made in China 2025: Die Kampfansage an Deutschland* [Online]. Available at: https://www.zeit.de/wirtschaft/2015-05/china-industrie-technologie-innovation [Accessed: 5 May 2018].

Wübbeke, J., Zenglein, M.J., Meissner, M., Conrad, B. and Ives, J. (2016). *Made in China 2025 - The Making of a High-Tech Superpower and Consequences for Industrial Countries.* Berlin: Mercator Institute for China Studies. Available at: https://www.merics.org/en/papers-on-china/made-china-2025 [Accessed: 25 May 2018].

Zakaria, F., Ferguson, N., Kissinger, H. and Li, D.D. (2011). *Does the Twenty-First Century Belong to China?* 1st ed. Toronto: Anansi Press.

Zand, B. (2015). Weltwirtschaft: Weg von der Werkbank. *Der Spiegel* [Online] **34**. Available at: http://www.spiegel.de/spiegel/print/d-138148081.html [Accessed: 30 April 2018].

Zhong R. (2018). *For the U.S. and China, a Technology Cold War That's Freezing Over* [Online]. Available at: https://cn.nytimes.com/business/20180326/trump-china-tariffs-tech-cold-war/ [Accessed: 29 August 2018].